DEMOCRACY

DIANE BAILEY

MASON CREST
PHILADELPHIA

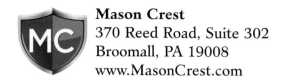

Mason Crest
370 Reed Road, Suite 302
Broomall, PA 19008
www.MasonCrest.com

Printed and bound in the United States of America

CPSIA Compliance Information: Batch #MEG2012-2. For further information, contact Mason Crest at 1-866-MCP-Book.

First printing
1 3 5 7 9 8 6 4 2

Library of Congress Cataloging-in-Publication Data

Bailey, Diane, 1966-
Democracy / Diane Bailey.
    p. cm. — (Major forms of world government)
Includes bibliographical references and index.
ISBN 978-1-4222-2137-2 (hc)
ISBN 978-1-4222-9454-3 (ebook)
1. Democracy—Juvenile literature. I. Title.
JC423.B1944 2013
321.8—dc23
                                2012027844

Publisher's note: All quotations in this book are taken from original sources, and contain the spelling and grammatical inconsistencies of the original texts.

TITLES IN THIS SERIES

COMMUNISM	MILESTONES	MONARCHY
DEMOCRACY	IN THE EVOLUTION	OLIGARCHY
DICTATORSHIP	OF GOVERNMENT	THEOCRACY
FASCISM		

TABLE OF CONTENTS

INTRODUCTION by Dr. Timothy Colton, Harvard University

When human beings try to understand complex sets of things, they usually begin by sorting them into categories. They classify or group the phenomena that interest them into boxes that are basically very much alike. These boxes can then be compared and analyzed. The logic of classification applies to the study of inanimate objects (such as, for example, bodies of water or minerals), to living organisms (such as species of birds or bacteria), and also to man-made systems (such as religions or communications media).

This series of short books is about systems of government, which are specific and very important kinds of man-made systems. Systems of government are arrangements for human control and cooperation on particular territories. Governments dispense justice, make laws, raise taxes, fight wars, run school and health systems, and perform many other services that we often take for granted. Like, say, minerals, bacteria, and religions, systems of government come in a wide variety of forms or categories.

Just what are those categories? One of the earliest attempts to answer this question rigorously was made in the fourth century BCE by the brilliant Greek philosopher Aristotle. His study *Politics* has come down to us in incomplete form, as many of his writings were lost after he died. Nonetheless, it contains a simple and powerful scheme for classifying systems of government. Aristotle researched and illustrated his treatise by looking at the constitutions of 158 small city-states near the eastern shores of the Mediterranean Sea of his day, most of them inhabited by Greeks.

According to Aristotle's *Politics*, any system of government could be accurately classified and thus understood once two things were known. The first was, how many people were involved in making political decisions: one person, a small number, or a large number. The second issue was whether the system was designed to serve the common good of the citizens of the city-state. Taken together, these distinctions produced six categories of governmental system in all: monarchy (rule by one civic-minded person); tyranny (rule by one selfish person); aristocracy (rule by the few in the interests of all); oligarchy (rule by the few to suit themselves); constitutional government or "polity" (rule by the many in the common interest); and finally a form of mob rule (rule by the many with no concern for the greater good).

The fifth of these classic categories comes closest to modern representative democracy, as it is experienced in the United States, Western Europe, India, and many other places. One of the things Aristotle teaches us, however, is that there are many alternatives to this setup. In addition to the volume on democracy, this Mason Crest series will acquaint students with systems of government that correspond in rough terms to other categories invented by Aristotle more than two thousand years ago. These include monarchy; dictatorship (in Aristotle's terms, tyranny); oligarchy; communism (which we might think of as a particular kind of modern-day oligarchy); fascism (which combines some of the characteristics of tyranny and mob rule); and theocracy (which does not fit easily into Aristotle's scheme, although we might think of it as tyranny or oligarchy, but in the name of some divine being or creed).

Aristotle focused his research on the written constitutions of city-states. Today, political scientists, with better tools at their disposal, delve more into the actual practice of government in different countries. That practice frequently differs from the theory written into the constitution. Scholars study why it is that countries differ so much in terms of how and in whose interests governmental decisions are taken, across broad categories and within these categories, as well as in mixed systems that cross the boundaries between categories. It turns out that there are not one but many reasons for these differences, and there are significant disagreements about which reasons are most important. Some of the reasons are examined in this book series.

Experts on government also wonder a lot about trends over time. Why is it that some version of democracy has come to be the most common form of government in the contemporary world? Why has democratization come in distinct waves, with long periods of stagnation or even of reverse de-democratization separating them? The so-called third wave of democratization began in the 1970s and extended into the 1990s, and featured, among other changes, the collapse of communist systems in the Soviet Union and Eastern Europe and the disintegration of differently constituted nondemocratic systems in Southern Europe and Latin America. At the present time, the outlook for democracy is uncertain. In a number of Arab countries, authoritarian systems of government have recently been overthrown or challenged by revolts. And yet, it is far from clear that the result will be functioning democracies. Moreover, it is far from clear that the world will not encounter another wave of de-democratization. Nor can we rule out the rise of fundamentally new forms of government not foreseen by Aristotle; these might be encouraged by contemporary forms of technology and communication, such as the Internet, behavioral tracking devices, and social media.

For young readers to be equipped to consider complex questions like these, they need to begin with the basics about existing and historical systems of government. It is to meet their educational needs that this book series is aimed.

Nelson Mandela, president of the African National Congress (ANC), casts his vote in South Africa's first truly democratic elections, April 1994.

1

A PEOPLE'S GOVERNMENT

Democracy wasn't the inspired invention of some brilliant individual. It didn't spring up fully formed or sweep rapidly across the globe once introduced. The basic ideas underpinning democracy —that government exists for the benefit of the people, and that it must have their consent to be legitimate—may seem obvious today. But such was not the case throughout most of human history.

AUTHORITARIAN RULE THROUGH THE AGES

Historically, coercion rather than consent was the governing principle in most civilizations. Individual rulers or a small ruling class wielded near-absolute power. They demanded obedience from their subjects. They used violence or the threat of violence to maintain social control.

Many leaders didn't bother to offer justifications for their right to rule. Military power made the question of legitimacy irrelevant. On the other hand, the absolute rulers of the past often claimed that their authority was divinely sanctioned. The pharaohs of ancient Egypt and the Inca emperors of Peru, for instance, were considered gods in their own right. Chinese emperors ruled under the so-called Mandate of Heaven. According to this idea, Heaven granted the emperor supreme power to govern. However, if the emperor abused his power, Heaven's blessing would be withdrawn. Evidence that the emperor had lost the Mandate of Heaven might include natural disasters such as droughts, floods, or crop failures, or even widespread social strife. In such cases, the emperor could justifiably be overthrown (and, in fact, a successful rebellion constituted proof that the deposed sovereign had forfeited Heaven's blessing). By contrast, medieval European monarchs didn't acknowledge

Golden statue of the last Incan emperor, Atahualpa (1497–1533), in Cuzco, Peru. In many ancient civilizations, including that of South America's Incas, the ruler was considered a god whose word was law and whose decisions could not be challenged.

any circumstances under which their removal from power was justified. They claimed, under a doctrine known as the divine right of kings, that their rule was the expression of God's will. Hence opposition to the monarch amounted to disobedience of God himself.

Exceptions to the pattern of authoritarian governance were, until relatively recent times, fairly rare. Still, the world's first known democracy flourished, albeit briefly, some 2,500 years ago.

RULE BY THE PEOPLE

The English word *democracy* comes from *demokratia*, an ancient Greek term formed by the combination of *demos*, meaning "the people"; and *kratos*, meaning "power" or "rule." Thus democracy is rule by the people. It is a form of government in which power ultimately resides with all citizens, rather than with an individual (as, for example, in an absolute monarchy), a small group (as in an oligarchy), or a single political party (as in a Communist state).

In a democracy, the people exercise their power through participation in the political process. Democracies offer citizens the chance to vote, or to run for public office, in regularly held elections.

Of course, elections alone do not a democracy make. Most dictatorships hold elections. However, they use unfair and undemocratic means to ensure the results they want. Perhaps the most straightforward way to rig an election is through electoral fraud—for example, by destroying ballots cast for an opponent. Another common tool is the use of police or military forces to intimidate voters and harass opposition candidates.

In some countries the barriers to democracy are structural. In Cuba, for example, citizens vote

KEY IDEA

Democracy is founded on the idea that a nation's people have the right to decide how they will be governed. The people express their will through elections.

THE ROAD TO UNIVERSAL SUFFRAGE

Today universal suffrage—the right of all adult citizens to vote—is regarded as a requirement for any democracy. In the past, however, democracies excluded entire classes of people.

In 1789, when George Washington was elected the first president of the United States, voting was limited to adult white males who owned property. By the 1820s, most property requirements had been eliminated. Still, neither women nor blacks could vote.

African-American men finally received the right to vote in 1870, with the ratification of the Fifteenth Amendment to the U.S. Constitution. But southern states soon found ways to prevent blacks from exercising their voting rights, including poll taxes and literacy tests. Only with the Voting Rights Act of 1965 would these barriers finally be removed.

By the late 1800s, women had limited voting rights in several countries. In 1893 New Zealand became the first nation to extend full voting rights to women. The United States achieved that milestone in 1920, when the Nineteenth Amendment was ratified. British women wouldn't receive equal voting rights with men until 1928. In France, female suffrage began in 1944. Switzerland didn't grant women the right to vote until 1971.

Suffragists picket outside the White House in 1917, demanding the right to vote. American women would be granted the vote with ratification of the Nineteenth Amendment in 1920.

for members of the legislature—the National Assembly—which in turn elects the country's president and vice president. However, candidates for the National Assembly always get 100 percent of the vote, because they run unopposed. The candidates are selected by the Communist Party, the only legal political party in Cuba. Iran's constitution requires all would-be candidates for office to receive the approval of an unelected 12-member committee of Islamic legal authorities known as the Council of Guardians. In 2009 it rejected nearly 500 presidential aspirants, permitting just four candidates on the ballot.

In a true democracy, the opportunity to run for public office cannot be limited to members of a ruling party, or to candidates with views acceptable to those in power. Voters must have real choices. Democracy emphasizes robust competition.

Democracy also emphasizes inclusion. Today, universal suffrage—the right of all adult citizens to vote—is generally regarded as a requirement for democracy. Historically, that wasn't the case, however. Until the 20th century, almost every democratic country failed to extend voting rights to women.

Another requirement for democracy is the rule of law. Basically, what this means is that no one is above the law. This includes top leaders, who must obey the law just like everyone else.

LIBERAL DEMOCRACY

Free, fair, and open elections. The right of all, or nearly all, adult citizens to vote. The rule of law. If these conditions are met, a country may be said to have an electoral democracy.

But when people today think of democracy, they usually have a broader concept in mind: liberal democracy. Liberal democracy involves not simply the process by which citizens select their government. It also involves how the government functions, and even what the purpose of government is.

At the heart of liberal democracy is the idea that all people have certain fundamental rights. These include the right to express one's ideas and opinions freely; the right to follow the religion of one's choosing, or not to follow any religion at all; and the right to due process, or fair legal proceedings, when accused of a crime. Liberal democracies consider such rights innate. They aren't conferred on citizens by their government. Rather, everyone has these rights simply by virtue of being human. Nor can a government legitimately take away fundamental human rights. In fact, a crucial premise of liberal democracy is that governments are established for the express purpose of protecting these rights.

"I WOULD RATHER BE EXPOSED TO THE INCONVENIENCES ATTENDING TOO MUCH LIBERTY THAN TO THOSE ATTENDING TOO SMALL A DEGREE OF IT."

—THOMAS JEFFERSON

While all governments compel citizens to follow certain rules—society couldn't function otherwise—liberal democracies put a high value on liberty. Within the bounds of the law, individuals in a liberal democracy are free to live their lives as they see fit. And it makes no difference whether most people disapprove of an individual's choices. The will of the majority may determine the outcome of elections in liberal democracies, but the fundamental rights of minorities are nevertheless protected.

* * * * *

Today the idea of democracy enjoys very wide acceptance. Even dictators feel compelled to pay lip service to governing with the consent of the governed. But the path to government by the people has been a long and difficult one.

2

ANCIENT ORIGINS

Greece has traditionally been credited as the birthplace of democracy. The Greek city-state of Athens introduced democratic governance around 500 BCE.

But some scholars suggest that democracy first developed much earlier, and in a different region: Mesopotamia. Located in modern-day Iraq, Mesopotamia is home to some of the world's oldest civilizations. Records written on clay tablets reveal that by the third millennium BCE, city-states in Mesopotamia had assemblies. These assemblies weren't permanent bodies. They appear to have met in times of emergency and, in some cases, when large-scale public-works projects were planned. It's unclear who sat on the assemblies or what the exact scope of their powers was.

The world's oldest known epic poem might shed some light on the matter. *Gilgamesh* tells the story of a king of Uruk, a city-state of the Sumerian civilization. The epic is believed to have been inspired by the life of an actual king of Uruk who ruled around 2700 BCE. In the epic, Uruk is threatened by the armies of another city-state. Gilgamesh, the king, consults two groups before deciding whether to wage war or try to make peace. One is a council of Uruk's male elders. The other is an assembly of Uruk's fighting men. Does this incident indicate that some form of democracy existed in actual Sumerian society? Some scholars say yes. They doubt the epic would describe the king seeking consent to go to war if there were no historical basis for that detail. And if their assemblies had authority on such important matters as war and peace, couldn't Sumerian city-states accurately be described as having at least a basic form of democracy?

Most experts don't think so. Early Mesopotamian rulers may sometimes have bowed to the will of assemblies. But there is scant evidence that they were required to do so. Nor is there evidence that ordinary people partici-

pated. The assemblies may well have been composed entirely of members of a noble class. Thus most scholars believe early Mesopotamia had a primitive form of oligarchy rather than a simple kind of democracy.

Mesopotamia's early assemblies didn't lead to greater democracy. Later rulers in the region wielded absolute power. But assemblies were adopted by other cultures. Among them were the Phoenicians, a seafaring people who settled in the eastern Mediterranean

One of the earliest known systems of laws was promulgated by the Mesopotamian ruler Hammurabi some 3,700 years ago. The "Code of Hammurabi" was inscribed on a basalt stela in the Akkadian language. Hammurabi's laws formed the basis for government in the Babylonian empire that he ruled, setting out the rights and duties of his subjects.

region. Phoenician city-states were ruled by powerful kings. Yet Phoenician kings sometimes consulted with a council of elders—references to which date as far back as the 14th century BCE. Later, a few Phoenician city-states also developed a "people's assembly." It was apparently composed of free male citizens. As in Mesopotamia, though, it's unclear what powers the Phoenician council of elders or people's assembly actually exercised.

THE GREEKS

Around the ninth century BCE, independent city-states began to replace tribes as the dominant form of political organization on the Greek mainland. Over the succeeding centuries, Greek colonists also established city-states in southern Italy, Sicily and other Mediterranean islands, Asia Minor (modern-day Turkey), and the Black Sea region.

Many Greek city-states followed a similar pattern of development. At first, they were ruled by kings. But monarchy evolved into oligarchy as power shifted to a small number of noble families. These nobles ruled through councils and assemblies. The system served the interests of the aristocratic few. Common people weren't represented, and in many Greek city-states the oligarchy grew very unpopular.

Change began to come around the middle of the seventh century BCE. Enlisting the support of the lower classes in general or of a particular faction or clan, individuals in various Greek city-states took power by force. These men were called tyrants. Today the word *tyrant* usually refers to a brutal and oppressive dictator. That wasn't necessarily the case in ancient Greece. Some tyrants did in fact rule harshly. Others, however, were popular, capable, and moderate leaders. A tyrant simply was a man who had taken power unlawfully or in a way that went against tradition.

Greece's largest city-state, Athens, seemed ripe for takeover by a tyrant during the last decades of the seventh century. The aristocracy was driving more and more people into destitution. Small farmers often found it necessary to take out loans from wealthy aristocrats. The terms of these loans were hard: The lender was entitled to a sizeable percentage of the farmer's produce. If the farmer couldn't pay—as often occurred in years when the harvest wasn't good—the lender could enslave the farmer and take the land.

The lower classes had few options. The aristocracy kept a tight hold on political power through a council known as the Areopagus. It was composed entirely of aristocratic men. The Areopagus judged legal cases in Athens. Each year it also selected nine men, who were also always members of the noble class, to serve as *archons*, or magistrates. One archon held primary responsibility for running the Athenian government and creating laws. After their one-year term was over, archons became lifetime members of the Areopagus.

Athens also had a larger assembly, called an *ecclesia*. The Athenian Assembly was open to non-noble but wealthy citizens. It had little real authority, however.

SOLON'S REFORMS

In 594 BCE, amid social unrest and a worsening economic situation, the Areopagus appointed a poet named Solon as archon. He quickly canceled the debts of poor farmers and prohibited Athenians from enslaving other Athenians. Solon also reformed the political institutions of Athens. He made wealth rather than noble birth alone the requirement for membership in the Areopagus. Solon also made every Athenian citizen a member of the Assembly. He expanded its role somewhat—for example, by giving it a say in the selection of archons. Still, Solon's reforms kept most of the political power in the hands of the wealthy. Historians don't believe Solon was trying to establish democracy in Athens. His goal, rather, was to curb social unrest and prevent a tyrant from seizing power.

In spite of Solon's reforms, that happened. Backed by a force of bodyguards, a popular general named Pisistratus made himself tyrant of Athens in 560. Pisistratus was soon driven out of the city. He returned and ruled for a few years, only to be driven out once more. In 546 Pisistratus assembled a large army and returned to Athens yet again. This time he managed to hold on to power. Pisistratus maintained a private army, exiled his opponents, and made sure only his supporters served as archons. Nevertheless, he was quite popular. He restricted the privileges of the aristocracy, redistributing some of their land to the poor. His trade policies brought increased prosperity. Pisastratus was also a great patron of the arts and culture.

Upon his death in 528 or 527, Pisistratus was succeeded by his sons, Hippias and Hipparchus. For a while, their rule was benign. After his brother was assassinated, however, Hippias became extremely repressive. An exiled noble family moved to overthrow him, but this effort failed. Eventually, the Athenian nobles secured the aid of another Greek city-state, Sparta. The Spartan army finally overthrew Hippias in 510.

A GOLDEN AGE OF DEMOCRACY

In 508 a noble named Cleisthenes came to power in Athens. Building on the earlier reforms of Solon, he would chart a democratic course for the city-state.

Recognizing that tyrants often exploited clan rivalries, Cleisthenes reorganized the political divisions of Athens. He

The Athenian lawmaker Solon (638–558 BCE) proposed reforms intended to wrest power from the wealthy aristocratic class and give the common people of Athens a greater voice in government. Although his reforms failed to prevent a tyrant from taking power, they would help lay the foundation for Athenian democracy.

replaced the four traditional tribes, which were based on blood relation-ships, with 10 "tribes" based on area of residence. Each of the new tribes contributed 50 men to a 500-member council known as the Boule. It pro-posed laws to the Athenian Assembly. The Assembly could accept, reject, or send proposed laws back to the Boule for revisions. The Areopagus retained judicial powers. It also had the authority to safeguard the Athenian constitution. This apparently gave the council of former archons an effective veto over laws approved by the Assembly.

In the 460s, however, the Athenian leader Ephialtes succeeded in stripping the Areopagus of almost all of its authority. The powers formerly wielded by the Areopagus were divided among the Boule, the Assembly, and ordinary law courts. In 461 Ephialtes was assassinated in a plot to restore oligarchy to Athens. But his successor, Pericles, main-tained and even strengthened the reforms. Under Pericles' 30-year-long leadership, Athens experienced a golden age of democracy. The people ruled as never before.

In many respects, democracy as practiced in ancient Athens bears little resemblance to the democracy we know today. The Athenian system was a form of "direct democracy." Citizens didn't elect lawmakers to represent them. Rather, citizens had the right to vote directly on all proposed laws. They exercised this right in the Assembly, which was open to all male citi-zens over age 18 who had completed two years of military service. Anyone present could speak in favor of or against a law. A majority of votes meant the measure passed. The Assembly met about 40 times per year.

The Boule, which set the agenda for the Assembly and also ensured that its decisions were carried out, was staffed with 50 men from each of the 10 tribes. They were picked at random from the pool of citizens age 30 and older. The same method was used to fill administrative posts in Athens. Terms of service were for one year, and no one could serve more than once in the same administrative post (twice in the Boule). All of this was designed to prevent corruption and other abuses of power. But it also reflected the Athenian belief in equality. No one was more or less fit to participate in government. Public service was a right and responsibility of all male citizens. To ensure that poor Athenians could serve without undue hardship, Pericles introduced the practice of paying officeholders.

The justice system was another reflection of the Athenian ideals of equality and citizen participation. Athens had no professional police force. It had no professional prosecutors. Ordinary citizens brought charges against fellow citizens. Trials were held without lawyers or judges. The accused and the accuser argued their case in front of a jury of citizens. Juries were large—500 or more—and were chosen by lot from a 6,000-man jury pool that was also chosen by lot. As with other public posts, jurors served for one year, and they received payment so that poor citizens could participate.

A few positions in the Athenian democracy weren't chosen by lot because they were deemed to require special skills or talents. These included the position of *strategos* (general). Each year the Assembly elected 10 generals (one from each tribe). They were responsible for overseeing foreign affairs, maintaining military readiness, planning strategy, and leading forces in battle. The 10 generals had equal status. Supreme command rotated daily. Generals could be reelected annually. But they could also be removed by the Assembly for failure to fulfill their duties adequately. And in that case they might face punishment ranging from a fine to execution.

The 30-year period during which Pericles (ca. 495–429 BCE) ruled Athens is considered a "golden age" for the city and its democratic government.

Athens had another unusual method for ensuring that no general—or, for that matter, anyone else—would be tempted to grab power. It was called ostracism. If citizens believed that a person was undermining the democracy, a vote would be held in the Assembly. If enough voters agreed, the person would be banished from Athens for 10 years. Ostracism appears to have been used only rarely, however.

THE LIMITS OF GREEK DEMOCRACY

Athens during the fifth century BCE attained a remarkable degree of democracy. Everyone had to follow the law, regardless of social station. Rich and poor citizens alike participated directly in the governance of their society.

Government by the people proved an attractive ideal for other Greek city-states as well. Many, though not all, followed Athens in establishing democracies.

But the achievements of Greek democracy, while impressive, must be kept in perspective. A relatively small proportion of the population had any voice in civic affairs. In Athens this figure was no more than 20 percent. To begin with, all women were excluded from participating in the political process. So, too, was anyone not born in Athens and anyone with a parent who wasn't an Athenian citizen. These people could never become citizens. Then there were slaves, who made up at least a quarter of the population.

In its foreign policy, Athens sought to be the Greek world's dominant power. This brought it into conflict with Sparta, and in 431 BCE the Peloponnesian War broke out. Twenty years later, with the grueling war still going on, the Athenian democracy was overthrown in a coup. The brutal oligarchy that gained power executed many supporters of democracy. But within a year, democracy had been restored. Sparta finally won the Peloponnesian War in 404. It helped install another harsh oligarchy in defeated Athens. Once again, however, Athenians soon ousted the ruling oligarchs and reestablished citizen self-government.

Democracy in Athens and other city-states in Greece continued well into the fourth century BCE. In 338 the king of neighboring Macedon,

In the Roman Republic, the motto SPQR represented an abbreviation of the Latin phrase *Senatus Populusque Romanus*, meaning "The Senate and the People of Rome." The SPQR inscription, which indicated that Roman citizens held political power in the republic, appeared on coins and government documents, was carved into buildings and monuments, and decorated the flags that Roman armies carried into battle.

Philip II, conquered Greece. Philip and his son, Alexander the Great, snuffed out the Greek experiment with democracy.

THE RISE OF ROME

As Greek civilization declined, the influence of another Mediterranean civilization—Rome—was on the rise. By 265 BCE, after more than two centuries of expansion, Rome controlled the entire Italian peninsula. Its campaign of empire building, however, was just beginning.

Rome had a republican form of government. In other words, its citizens exercised political power not directly, as in Athens, but by electing officials to represent them and run the state. The actual extent of citizen self-government in the Roman Republic was limited, however. For example, the decisions of an elected assembly were supposed to be binding. The unelected Senate—composed largely of aristocrats—was, in theory, simply an advisory body. However, Senate decrees often determined policy.

In the first century BCE, the Roman Republic ended. It was replaced by the rule of emperors whose personal authority was nearly unlimited—as long as they maintained the support of the army.

3

EVOLVING INSTITUTIONS

The Roman Empire was vast. At its greatest extent, it covered much of Europe; a swath of North Africa, including Egypt; the eastern Mediterranean region; and Asia Minor. The empire was no democracy. But it did bequeath to the world something that would prove vital to the later development of democracy: a highly developed system of law.

The Roman tradition recognized different categories of law. In Roman legal thinking, civil law is the law a society creates for its own government. Civil law not only varies from one society to another, but also changes over time. Civil law is written law, and it must be made publicly known.

Natural law, by contrast, consists of eternal principles that are binding on all societies. These principles can serve as a foundation for human-made laws. "The laws of nature, which all nations observe alike, being established by a divine providence, remain ever fixed and immutable," a group of legal scholars wrote when Roman law was codified under the emperor Justinian. "But the laws which every state has enacted, undergo frequent changes, either by the tacit consent of the people, or by a new law being subsequently passed."

It followed from the Roman conception of natural law that all people might possess certain universal rights. This was a very important concept. So, too, was the idea that the consent of the people might play a role in the evolution of a government's laws.

MEDIEVAL EUROPE

In 395 CE, the Roman Empire was divided into western and eastern halves. The Eastern Roman Empire was centered in Constantinople (modern-day Istanbul, Turkey). The Western Roman Empire, centered in Rome, collapsed in the fifth century. Afterward, Europe entered a period known as the Middle Ages. It lasted from around 500 to around 1500.

Hereditary monarchies, along with the powerful Catholic Church, dominated Europe during this period. That's not to say, however, that the democratic impulse was dead. For example, from at least the 700s, assemblies of free men met periodically in parts of Viking Scandinavia. At these assemblies, known as *things*, laws were confirmed, disputes resolved, and, in some cases, kings elected. Later, during the 11th and 12th centuries, certain towns in northern Italy had elected councils as well as assemblies that were open to all male citizens. But in all of these towns, noble families eventually took control. Fledgling democratic institutions were replaced with oligarchies.

If the Middle Ages failed to produce any large-scale or stable democracy, it did witness a gradual trend toward the curbing of absolute authority. By the ninth century, a system commonly known as feudalism had begun to emerge in Europe. Under this system, kings leased land (called fiefdoms) and provided protection to high-ranking noble lords. In return, the lords swore loyalty to the king and raised military forces for him. Higher-ranking lords, in turn, leased land to lower-ranking nobles and offered them protection. The lower-ranking nobles owed allegiance to the more powerful lord. At the bottom of the system were landless peasants called serfs. They lived on and worked the land of the local nobleman, to whom they owed labor and taxes.

Feudal society, though hierarchical, involved a great deal of interdependency. While he stood at the top of the political, social, and military order, a king needed the cooperation of his lords. He couldn't afford to alienate them completely. If they united against him, he would not be on the throne for long.

THE GREAT CHARTER

From around the 600s to the 1110s, kings in England consulted from time to time with a council called the *witenagemot*. It was composed of the most important nobles and church officials in the kingdom. The witenagemot appears to have played a mostly advisory role. The king alone had the power to convene it. He could also choose to follow or ignore its counsel.

In the late 11th century, the witenagemot was replaced by the *Curia Regis* ("king's court"). Made up of high-ranking nobles, church leaders, and royal advisers, this appointed council helped the king of England administer his realm. Over hundreds of years, the Curia Regis would grow into Parliament, the English legislature.

One key event came in 1100, when King Henry I claimed the throne following the death of his older brother, King William II. William had been highly unpopular with church officials and with England's nobility. Seeking to gain the support of these groups, Henry issued the Charter of Liberties. In it the king promised to treat church officials and nobles according to specified rules.

The Charter of Liberties was the forerunner of a more important document. In 1215 King John signed the Magna Carta ("Great Charter"). It affirmed that the king, like everyone else, had to obey the law of the land. He couldn't exercise power arbitrarily. His subjects—at least those who weren't serfs—had rights and liberties. One clause of the Magna Carta read:

No free man shall be seized or imprisoned, or stripped of his rights or possessions, or outlawed or exiled, or deprived of his standing in any other way, nor will we proceed with force against him, or send others to do so, except by the lawful judgement of his equals or by the law of the land.

Though its primary focus was on securing the rights of England's high-ranking nobles, the Magna Carta's limitation of royal power was a crucial step toward democracy. Ironically, this step was taken in a most undemocratic way. Many barons were angry at John's abuses of power. When discussions with the king failed to resolve their grievances, the barons drew up the Magna Carta, cornered John in a field, and forced him to sign the document. "Except for a tiny handful of cases," the political scientist John Keane writes in *The Life and Death of Democracy*, "democracy has never been built democratically. Historical records show that its invention does not happen overnight, and that it has causes and causers. It rarely springs from the clear-headed intentions and clean hands of people using democratic means."

The Magna Carta didn't survive untouched. Several versions were issued during the 13th century, with parts of the original repealed or modified. Still, the shift in power away from the monarchy and toward the people had begun.

THE MODEL PARLIAMENT

Democracy would get another boost in 1295. That year, King Edward I summoned a council. He wanted help in raising money for military campaigns in Scotland and elsewhere. As with past councils, this one included lords representing the interests of the landed nobility, as well as bishops representing the interests of the church and

King John signs the Magna Carta, one of the most important documents in the history of democracy.

clergy. However, Edward also decreed that the council include a greater cross-section of society. Knights from each county were to elect two of their own to send to the council. Likewise, the citizens of each borough and each city were to choose two men for the council. These men weren't necessarily wealthy or educated (though no peasants were included). They came from the Commons—the class of ordinary people.

Edward's council would be dubbed the "Model Parliament." Though it was a unified body, its composition of nobles and commoners would set the stage for Britain's two-chamber Parliament, consisting of the House of Lords and the House of Commons. The English parliamentary system would take hundreds of years to evolve. But the Model Parliament of 1295 presaged a major trend: the assertiveness of the Commons. Edward had wanted a rubber stamp for higher taxation. But the commoners in the Model Parliament insisted that he address certain grievances before they would agree to raise money for his wars.

STRUGGLE FOR AUTHORITY

Similar developments were taking place elsewhere in Europe. In France, for example, King Philip IV summoned the "Estates-General" for the first time in 1302. The Estates-General was composed of representatives of the clergy, the nobility, and the bourgeoisie (prosperous residents of France's growing towns and cities). Philip wanted—and received—approval from the Estates-General for his power struggle with the pope. But throughout the 14th century, other Estates-General proved unwilling to bend to the will of the monarch.

In France, England, and elsewhere, the early forays into a more democratic decision-making process proved unstable. Monarchs called parliaments, estates-general, and other assemblies because they wanted support for their policies, particularly schemes to raise more revenue. But the assemblies often had a different agenda. The contest for power played out differently in different countries. In France, the monarchy had won out by the 16th century. Estates-General were no longer consulted, and the king wielded absolute power. In Britain, struggles between Parliament and the king led to the English Civil War (1642–1651). The forces of Parliament prevailed. King Charles I was executed, his heir exiled, and the monarchy replaced by a republican government, the Commonwealth. The Commonwealth was short lived, however. In 1653 a leader of the Parliamentary military forces, Oliver Cromwell, had himself named Lord Protector. Cromwell exerted near-dictatorial authority until his death in 1658. Two years later, the British monarchy was restored.

England's Parliament and king were again at loggerheads by the 1680s. The trouble involved religion. King James II was Catholic, while most Britons were Protestants. James's daughter Mary, a Protestant married to the Dutch ruler William of Orange, was in line for the British throne until James fathered a son in 1688. Fearing a Catholic dynasty, Parliament invited William of Orange to invade England and overthrow King James. He did. This event, part of what became known as the Glorious Revolution, marked a turning point in British political development. Parliament in 1689 passed the Bill of Rights. It established, once and for all, that British monarchs needed the assent of Parliament to govern. The Bill of Rights required the monarch to get Parliament's approval in order to impose new taxes or to keep a standing army in peacetime. It prohibited royal interference in the election of members of Parliament. And it outlawed the imposition of "cruel and unusual" punishments on any subject.

A constitutional framework of governance had been established, and Parliament's authority was clearly on the rise. Still, the British monarchy retained significant powers. All laws passed by Parliament were subject to the approval of the king or queen. Peerages—hereditary titles of nobility that entitled someone to sit in the House of Lords—were bestowed by the monarchy. And the House of Lords had to give its assent to any new law. Only the House of Commons was elected, and only Protestant male property owners—a small percentage of the population—had the right to vote. So it would be inaccurate to say that Britain in the wake of the Glorious Revolution had a democracy. But the political developments in Britain would reverberate across the Atlantic Ocean, where another revolution would indeed lead to democracy.

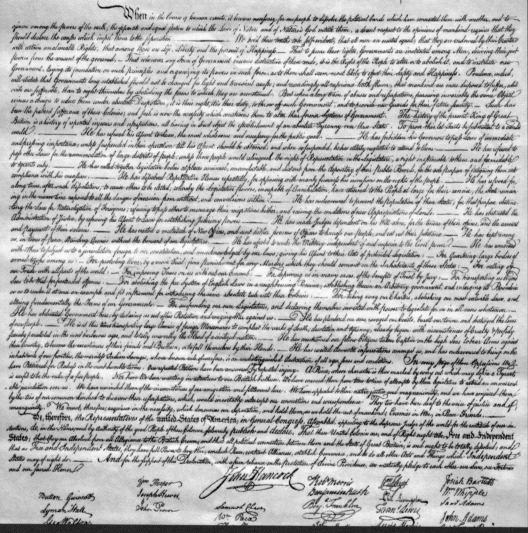

The Declaration of Independence sets out the democratic principles on which the United States of America would be founded: "We hold these truths to be self-evident, that all men are created equal, that they are endowed by their Creator with certain unalienable Rights, that among these are Life, Liberty and the pursuit of Happiness. — That to secure these rights, Governments are instituted among Men, deriving their just powers from the consent of the governed. — That whenever any Form of Government becomes destructive of these ends, it is the Right of the People to alter or to abolish it, and to institute new Government, laying its foundation on such principles and organizing its powers in such form, as to them shall seem most likely to effect their Safety and Happiness."

4

THE AMERICAN WAY

During the 1600s and early 1700s, English set-
tlers established colonies in eastern North
America. There would eventually be 13 of
these colonies. Their governments varied. Most
had governors appointed by—and representing
the interests of—the British monarch. Governors,
in turn, appointed members to a council. These
councils typically had extensive powers, including
the authority to reject new laws and the authority
to act as a supreme court.

As in Britain, the colonies also had elected
assemblies. To be eligible to vote, a colonist had to
be free, white, male, and a property owner. Usually
the colonial assemblies met once a year, and for just
a couple weeks. Although their legislative acts
needed approval from the governor and the council, the assemblies had sole authority over taxation.

Colonial courts operated under the British system of common law, and the colonists were subjects of the Crown. But thanks to the structure of colonial governments, they enjoyed a measure of self-government.

ENLIGHTENED IDEAS

From the late 1600s through the 1700s, as the British North American colonies were growing and developing, a wide-ranging philosophical movement known as the Enlightenment swept across Europe. The Enlightenment emphasized reason, science, and freedom of thought. It challenged tradition, religious faith, and superstition as appropriate foundations for human behavior—or for governmental authority.

With regard to democratic governance, two of the most important Enlightenment philosophers were John Locke (1632–1704) and Charles-Louis de Secondat, Baron de Montesquieu (1689–1755). Locke, an Englishman, said that all people have natural rights—life, liberty, health, and property. These rights are "inalienable." In other words, they can't justly be taken away or surrendered. In Locke's view, a government's legitimacy comes only from the consent of the governed. The primary role of government, according to Locke, is to protect the rights of citizens. He believed governments should give individuals the greatest amount of freedom compatible with a functioning society.

The English philosopher John Locke wrote that all men are created equal. A fundamental aspect of democratic government is that the political system must treat every citizen the same. Each citizen gets one vote, and all votes are counted equally.

Montesquieu, a Frenchman, shared that belief. He wondered how

In his 1748 book *The Spirit of the Laws*, the French political philosopher Montesquieu argued for distributing the powers of government among three branches (executive, legislative, and judicial), each with specific responsibilities. This, he said, was the best way to ensure that the rights and freedoms of individual citizens would be protected. Montesquieu's writings had a great influence on America's Founding Fathers.

liberty might be safeguarded. The solution, Montesquieu thought, was a framework that spread governing authority across different branches of government. This is called the separation of powers. Montesquieu identified three main administrative powers of government—legislative (the power to enact laws), executive (the power to implement laws), and judicial (the power to apply the law and judge legal disputes). No government official or group of officials, Montesquieu believed, should be able to exercise more than one of these powers. In a political work from 1748, he wrote:

> When the legislative and executive powers are united in the same person, or in the same body of magistrates, there can be no liberty . . . lest the same monarch or senate should enact tyrannical laws, to execute them in a tyrannical manner.

> Again, there is no liberty, if the power of judging be not separated from the legislative and executive powers. Were it joined with the legislative, the life and liberty of the subject would be exposed to arbitrary control, for the judge would then be the legislator. Were it joined to the executive power, the judge might behave with all the violence of an oppressor.

Educated people in the British North American colonies were familiar with Enlightenment ideas. Those ideas would play a major role in the creation of a new nation.

FRICTION IN THE COLONIES

In 1765 the British Parliament passed the Stamp Act. It imposed a new tax on printed materials in the North American colonies. The money raised from the tax was supposed to help replenish the royal treasury. Great Britain had just fought a long and expensive war, partly to protect the North American colonies from French incursion. In the view of British leaders, it wasn't unreasonable to expect the colonists to pay some of the costs for their own defense.

The colonists saw the matter differently. They believed they could be taxed only with their consent. They gave that consent through their representatives in the colonial assemblies. The colonists didn't get to vote for members of Parliament. Thus Parliament had no right to raise their taxes.

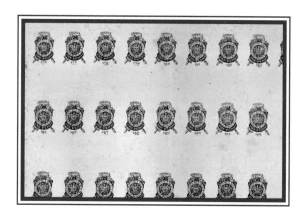

Under the Stamp Act of 1765, tax stamps like these were required on all legal documents, permits, contracts, newspapers, pamphlets, and playing cards in the American colonies. Parliament wanted to raise money to help pay for the cost of defending the colonies. Still, many Americans considered the stamp tax unfair because they were not represented in the British legislature.

Protests swept through the colonies. "No taxation without representation" became a rallying cry.

The Stamp Act was eventually repealed. But Parliament tried to impose other taxes on the colonies. Those taxes also met with stiff opposition. Relations between Britain and the colonists grew more and more tense.

In 1773 Parliament passed the Tea Act. It gave a royally chartered company a monopoly on the tea trade in the American colonies. Colonists chafed. In Philadelphia and New York,

British ships carrying tea were prevented from unloading their cargo. In Boston the reaction was even more confrontational. A group of colonists boarded ships at anchor and dumped more than 340 crates of tea into Boston Harbor.

In response, Parliament passed a series of measures that in the colonies would be called the Intolerable Acts. One closed the port of Boston. Others changed government and the administration of justice in Massachusetts. Towns now needed the royal governor's permission before they could hold meetings. Law enforcement officers had previously been elected, but now the governor appointed them. And appointed sheriffs were given the authority to choose jurors for trials. The governor was also empowered to send any official to England to face trial there.

Many Massachusetts colonists considered these measures violations of their rights as British subjects. But the Intolerable Acts were also broadly seen—in Massachusetts and the other colonies—as a threat to the natural rights of all colonists. In 1774 representatives of every colony except Georgia met in Philadelphia to discuss a response. The First Continental Congress, as this assembly was called, declared a boycott on goods imported from Britain. It also banned the export to Britain of most goods produced in the colonies.

Armed conflict finally erupted on April 19, 1775. That day, British soldiers and colonists clashed at Lexington and Concord, Massachusetts. The Revolutionary War had begun.

In June 1775 the Continental Congress authorized the creation of an army to fight the British forces. But many, if not most, colonists still considered themselves British subjects. They hoped their differences with the king and Parliament could be settled.

THE DECLARATION OF INDEPENDENCE

Any hope for reconciliation was ended by the early summer of 1776. On July 4, the Continental Congress adopted the Declaration of Independence. It announced that the colonies had dissolved their political

Members of the committee assigned to draft the Declaration of Independence—John Adams, Roger Sherman, Robert Livingston, Thomas Jefferson, and Benjamin Franklin—present the document to John Hancock, president of the Second Continental Congress, in June 1776.

connection with Great Britain and were now the free and independent "united States of America."

Written primarily by Thomas Jefferson, the Declaration of Independence carefully laid out the justification for the split with Great Britain. There were three essential parts. First, all humans have fundamental rights. Second, governments are set up to protect these rights, and they rule only with the consent of the people. Third, when a government violates the people's fundamental rights, the people have the right to get rid of that government and create another. As the Declaration famously states:

> We hold these Truths to be self-evident, that all Men are created equal, that they are endowed by their Creator with certain unalienable Rights, that among these are Life, Liberty, and the Pursuit of Happiness—That to secure these Rights, Governments are instituted among Men, deriving their just Powers from the Consent of the Governed, that whenever any Form of Government becomes destructive of these Ends, it is the Right of the People to alter or to abolish it, and to institute new Government.

This was a succinct and eloquent expression of the rationale for liberal democracy.

It took years for the Americans to actually win their freedom. The British surrender at Yorktown in October 1781 marked the end of major fighting. Two years later, a peace treaty was signed in Paris. It officially brought the Revolutionary War to an end, with Great Britain recognizing American independence.

TOWARD A MORE PERFECT UNION

The United States of America first operated under an agreement called the Articles of Confederation. It was passed by the Congress in 1777 and ratified by all the states in 1781.

American leaders feared that an overly powerful central government would lead to tyranny. So the Articles of Confederation left most power with the states. The weak central government didn't have an executive or judicial branch. And the Confederation Congress, the one-chamber national legislature, lacked the authority to tax, to regulate commerce, or even to enforce laws. To become binding on the states, any legislation passed by Congress had to receive the approval of at least 9 of the 13 states.

THE PENNSYLVANIA CONSTITUTION

Most American revolutionaries favored a national republican form of government that divided power. However, some states opted for a more basic form of democracy. The 1776 version of the Pennsylvania constitution stated, "There is but one rank of men in America . . . there should be only one representation of them in government." The Pennsylvanians rejected the idea of a governor and a senate, and instead created only one legislative body. In 1790, however, soon after the U.S. Constitution had been adopted, Pennsylvania changed its constitution to match the federal system.

THE ELECTORAL COLLEGE

The Electoral College system established by the Founding Fathers remains in place today. The number of electors each state receives is based on population. However, because the presidential candidate who wins the popular vote in a given state receives all that state's electoral votes (Maine and Nebraska are exceptions), it's possible for a presidential candidate to win the most votes nationwide but still lose the election. In fact, that has happened four times, most recently in 2000. In the 2000 election, Al Gore received over half a million more votes than George W. Bush, but Bush got 271 electoral votes to Gore's 266.

Problems with the Articles of Confederation became apparent in the postwar years. The states all maintained their own trade policies. Some printed their own currency. The United States was unable to raise funds to pay off its war debts. It lacked a strong national military.

Prominent Americans, including James Madison and Alexander Hamilton, began calling for a meeting to discuss ways to strengthen the national government. In late May 1787, delegates from all of the states except Rhode Island started arriving in Philadelphia for what became known as the Constitutional Convention. Over a period of four months, the 56 delegates—today referred to as the Founding Fathers—debated, quarreled, compromised, and ultimately hammered out the Constitution of the United States.

THE CONSTITUTION

The U.S. Constitution set up a federal republic. Under this system, political power would be divided between the states and the national, or federal, government.

At the federal level, the Founding Fathers adopted important aspects of the British system. Like Parliament, the U.S. Congress would be a bicameral (two-chamber) body. Members of the lower chamber, the House of Representatives, would be chosen by popular election. Members of the upper chamber, the Senate, would be appointed by their state legislatures. (This changed in 1913, with the ratification of the Seventeenth Amendment.) England's Parliament, too, had an elected lower chamber and an appointed upper chamber.

But America's Founding Fathers departed from the English model in critical ways. To begin, they opted for a more clear-cut separation of

The U.S. Constitution is a written document that embodies the fundamental principles of American government. All laws, actions by government leaders, and judicial decisions must conform to the Constitution.

OF CHECKS AND BALANCES

The U.S. Constitution has many safeguards against the concentration of political power. It provides for separate legislative, executive, and judicial branches of government. Furthermore, there are mechanisms by which each branch can curb the authority of the others. Called checks and balances, these measures help ensure that no branch will accumulate too much power. So, for example, in the United States the sole authority to create bills (proposed laws) at the federal level rests with Congress. But before a bill can become law, it must be submitted to the president. The president may veto, or reject, any bill. However, if a two-thirds majority in each chamber of Congress votes to override the president's veto, the bill becomes law anyway. Besides the executive-branch check provided by the veto, legislative power is restrained by the judicial branch. The courts have authority to strike down any law deemed to violate the U.S. Constitution, with the Supreme Court the final arbiter of constitutional disputes.

powers. Legislative and executive authority was intermingled in Britain, whose prime minister served both as head of government and as a member of the Parliament. By contrast, the U.S. Constitution created an independent executive branch. At its head was an elected president.

The Founding Fathers gave the president considerable power. But they vigorously rejected the idea that the president—or Congress, for that matter—could hold sovereign, or supreme, political authority. That belonged to the people. "The people are the King," delegate Gouverneur Morris said during one debate at the Constitutional Convention.

If the Founding Fathers embraced the essential idea of democracy, they also feared the consequences of too much democracy in practice. Many doubted that the majority of Americans had sufficient education to make wise decisions. They believed voters would be susceptible to manipulation by unscrupulous presidential candidates. As a safeguard against this, the Founding Fathers created the Electoral College. Voters casting their ballots for a presidential candidate would technically be voting for electors representing the candidate. These electors—prominent persons "most likely to possess the information and discernment requisite" for properly evaluating a candidate—would actually elect the president. In theory, the Electoral College might override the will of the majority of voters.

KEY IDEA

In 1791, 10 amendments were added to the U.S. Constitution. Known as the Bill of Rights, these amendments guarantee certain rights for U.S. citizens, including freedom of speech, freedom to assemble, freedom of religion, and the right to a trial by a jury. No laws can be made to override these rights.

A REPUBLIC

On September 17, 1787, delegates to the Constitutional Convention signed the final draft of the U.S. Constitution. Now 9 of the 13 states had to ratify the Constitution before it would go into effect. That occurred in June 1788.

The framework for government that the Founding Fathers had created would prove farsighted. Yet the Constitution wasn't perfect by any means. It didn't provide for participation in the political process by women. Even more glaring, it left intact the institution of slavery.

After the Constitutional Convention, a woman approached delegate Benjamin Franklin and asked what type of government had been decided upon. Franklin recognized that the proposed government was untried and would require the active efforts of citizens to sustain. Caution showed in his reply: "A republic, madam, if you can keep it."

5

GAINS AND SETBACKS

The United States did manage to keep its new republic. And the American experience would help inspire people in other countries to pursue democratic reforms.

THE FRENCH REVOLUTION

On May 5, 1789, France's king convened the Estates-General for the first time in 175 years. France was in the midst of financial difficulties. King Louis XVI hoped the Estates-General would approve higher taxes. Instead, delegates from the Third Estate—the commoners—declared themselves the National Assembly, representing the French people. They set about creating a constitution that would give the people broader rights. Eventually they were joined by some of the delegates from the First Estate (the clergy) and Second Estate (the nobility).

At first, Louis signaled that he would agree to a constitution drafted by the Assembly. But then he appeared to change his mind. On July 14, an angry mob in Paris seized the Bastille, a prison that was viewed as a symbol of royal power. The storming of the Bastille is generally said to mark the start of the French Revolution.

For a while, the Assembly maintained a guarded relationship with the monarchy, which didn't move to stop its work on a constitution. In August 1789 the Assembly got rid of France's feudal system, abolishing the special privileges of the clergy and the nobility. The Assembly also published the Declaration of the Rights of Man and the Citizen. Inspired by the American Declaration of Independence, it contained 17 articles. "Men are born and remain free and equal in rights," read the first article. "Social distinctions may be founded only upon the general good."

For more than two years, the Assembly worked to translate the general principles of the Declaration of the Rights of Man and the Citizen into a working constitution for the French government. Finally, in September 1791, the Assembly presented a constitution to the king, who agreed to accept it. The document created a constitutional monarchy. The single-chamber, elected Assembly would have most of the governing power, but the king would keep the authority to veto legislation and choose his ministers.

Anti-monarchical sentiment continued to run strong, however. In September 1792 the Assembly eliminated the monarchy and declared France a republic. The following January, Louis was executed for treason.

France's republic didn't last very long. In 1799 Napoleon Bonaparte staged a military coup. Napoleon made himself dictator and, in 1804, took the title Emperor of the French.

THE REVOLUTIONS OF 1848

Despite the untimely end of France's republican government, the French Revolution had planted seeds of change. In 1848 uprisings against authoritarian monarchs broke out across much of Europe. The Revolutions of 1848 began in France and spread to the German states, Austria, the

Italian states, Denmark, Hungary, and elsewhere. The specific issues that touched off the uprisings varied from place to place. In addition, the revolutionaries did little if anything to coordinate their efforts across national borders. But historians agree that the ideals of liberal democracy were an overarching inspiration for the revolutions. The revolutionaries demanded more freedoms and a greater voice in their governments.

Europe's monarchies, though shaken by the upheaval, managed to suppress the revolutions and reestablish their authority by 1849. "We have been beaten and humiliated," moaned the French philosopher and revolutionary Pierre-Joseph Proudhon. "We have been scattered, imprisoned, disarmed, and gagged. The fate of European democracy has slipped from our hands—from the hands of the people."

This illustration shows an angry mob tipping and burning a royal carriage at the Chateau d'Eu, France, 1848. That year, revolutions broke out in many countries of Europe, as well as in Latin America. For the most part, however, the revolutions failed to bring about meaningful democratic change.

Proudhon's bleak assessment wasn't entirely warranted. The revolutions brought an end to absolute monarchy in one country. In 1849 Frederick VII, the king of Denmark, signed a constitution that established a bicameral parliament and guaranteed certain rights and liberties, including freedom of speech. Switzerland and the Netherlands, though untouched by violence in 1848, also undertook major reforms. Switzerland's 1848 constitution created what was in essence (if not officially) a federal republic. Constitutional reforms in the Netherlands created a parliamentary democracy. Meanwhile, two other European countries, Great Britain and Belgium, were well on their way to becoming full-fledged liberal democracies—if they didn't already qualify for that designation.

MEASURING DEMOCRACY

How could there be any question as to whether, at a given point in time, a country does or does not qualify as a liberal democracy? To begin, a precise definition of the term *liberal democracy* is elusive. Political scientists agree on some—but by no means all—of the necessary attributes. Furthermore, these attributes tend not to be measurable in absolute terms but fall on a continuum.

For example, liberal democracies protect fundamental human rights such as freedom of speech. But every country places some limits on free speech. The United States draws a line at so-called fighting words—public expressions that might incite immediate violence. Yet the First Amendment to the Constitution protects all manner of offensive and hateful speech. Americans are allowed to give voice to racism, sexism, homophobia, religious bigotry, or any other prejudice. By contrast, many countries punish public utterances that demean an identifiable group of people. A partial list of such countries includes Brazil, Canada, Denmark, France, Germany, the Netherlands, Poland, Sweden, and the United Kingdom. Indonesia prohibits public expressions of hostility or contempt toward religion. Iran, Saudi Arabia, and Pakistan punish blasphemy, but only if it is directed at Islam. China punishes anyone who questions the legitimacy of the ruling Communist Party.

The question is, at what point do limits on free speech become too extensive for a country to be considered a liberal democracy? And, of course, freedom of expression is just one essential right. Liberal democracies are expected to protect a whole cluster of fundamental rights and liberties. Some governments might protect certain rights but not others. How should these governments be thought of?

In addition to the question of individual rights, issues surrounding the electoral process must be considered. Democracy requires free, fair, and open elections. But how are those qualities to be measured? For example, elections might not be feasible if everyone who wanted to run for office were automatically put on the ballot. But which sorts of eligibility requirements for candidates are reasonable and which are antidemocratic? What restrictions can a government legitimately place on voter eligibility?

As the above discussion indicates, deciding which countries qualify as liberal democracies and which do not isn't always a straightforward matter. The exercise can, in fact, be highly subjective.

Political scientists and democracy-advocacy organizations have developed an assortment of schemes that seek to measure objectively the various dimensions of democratic and authoritarian governments. One of the most widely cited is the Freedom in the World survey. It is produced by Freedom House, a nongovernmental organization based in Washington, D.C., that promotes democracy, political freedom, and human rights. The survey evaluates political rights and civil rights in all of the world's countries, using a scale of 1 (free) to 7 (not free). The scores for political rights and civil rights are averaged, yielding a measure of overall democratic freedoms. According to the Freedom House scale, a score of 1–2 means a country is free (and also a liberal democracy); a score of 3–5 means a country is partly free (and may qualify as an electoral democracy but not a liberal one); and and a score of 6–7 means a country is not free (and not democratic).

The Polity IV Project, which is affiliated with George Mason University in Virginia, provides another widely used scale for distinguishing liberal democratic and authoritarian governments. Polity IV is particularly useful for historical comparisons, as its data set gauges global trends in governance going back to 1800. Polity IV measures democratic and autocratic characteristics in a nation's governing institutions, with the overall score falling on a scale from -10 (hereditary monarchy) to +10 (consolidated democracy). Countries with a score between -10 and -6 are considered autocracies. Countries with a score of -5 to +5 are classified as "anocracies," or mixed-authority regimes. The threshold for a democracy is +6.

Russians line up to vote for president at a polling station in Ulan-Ude, March 2012. Although Russia holds democratic-style elections, few international observers regard the country as a true democracy. The Polity IV Project considers the Russian Federation as a "closed anocracy." A press release from the Organization for Security and Co-operation in Europe (OSCE), which monitors elections, enumerated some of the many undemocratic aspects of Russia's 2012 presidential balloting. In that election, the OSCE noted, Vladimir Putin's ultimate victory was never in doubt because voters' "choice was limited, electoral competition lacked fairness and an impartial referee was missing. . . . The point of elections is that the outcome should be uncertain. This was not the case in Russia. There was no real competition."

For the influential American political scientist Francis Fukuyama, three criteria are necessary for a liberal democracy. They are: a representative form of government; a market-based economy with strong protection of property rights; and a fair and strong system for administering justice.

DEMOCRACY SPREADS

By whichever scale is used, the latter half of the 19th century saw a rise in the number of democratic countries. Most of the new democracies were in western Europe. Many followed the British example of constitutional monarchy.

Constitutional monarchy is a form of government in which a king or queen functions as head of state, but with authority that is clearly defined and limited by a constitution. A constitutional monarchy is compatible with democratic governance.

In the case of Britain, the Glorious Revolution led to constitutional limits on the monarch's power. It also established the requirement of regular

MAJORITY/PLURALITY VS. PROPORTIONAL-REPRESENTATION VOTING

The world's democracies have a wide range of voting systems. However, most fall into one of two broad categories: majority/plurality or proportional representation.

The United States uses the majority/plurality system. In this system, voters cast their ballots for an individual candidate for office. The winner is the candidate who receives the most votes.

In proportional-representation systems, political parties put forth lists of candidates for office. Voters cast their ballots for their preferred party. The number of legislative seats each party is allotted is determined by the percentage of the vote the party receives.

elections for Parliament. But voting rights were too limited for Britain to be considered a democracy.

In 1832 Parliament passed the First Reform Act. It revamped Britain's electoral system. The act decreased the property requirements for men to vote. It also redistributed the seats in the House of Commons to more accurately reflect the population. Previously, so-called rotten boroughs—constituencies with very few voters—had been represented in the House of Commons, while growing industrial cities had no representation. For instance, in 1831 the village of Old Sarum in Wiltshire had just 15 residents but sent two members to the House of Commons. Meanwhile, not a single seat was reserved for Manchester, population 235,500.

Even after the First Reform Act, however, constituencies were of greatly unequal size. And even with the reduced property requirements, only about one in seven adult males was eligible to vote.

The Reform Act of 1867 further enlarged the pool of eligible voters. It specified that all male householders had the right to vote. So did men who rented rooms for at least £10 per year. This included many working-class men. Now, about 40 percent of adult males could vote.

As Britain expanded the franchise, so did other democratic countries. In the United States, the Fifteenth Amendment to the Constitution gave all African-American males the right to vote. With the 1870 ratification of the amendment, the franchise extended to all American men. In France all men were made eligible to vote in 1870 as well. Property requirements for Belgian men to vote were dropped in 1893.

By 1900, New Zealand—at the time a British possession—was the only place women were guaranteed the right to vote. Still, depending on the scale used, there were 10 or more liberal democracies in the world. Fukuyama lists 13: the United States, Canada, Switzerland, Great Britain, France, Belgium, the Netherlands, Denmark, Italy, Sweden, Greece, Chile, and Argentina. Liberal democracies continued to be clustered in Europe, with nine representatives.

But if European nations increasingly accepted the right of citizens to determine how they would be governed, those nations didn't necessarily respect the will of the people in other parts of the world. Democratic countries such as Great Britain and France carved out large overseas empires. Local peoples under colonial rule in Africa, Asia, and elsewhere weren't allowed to choose their own system of government.

BATTLEGROUND EUROPE

In August 1914, Europe was engulfed in a huge conflict that history knows as World War I. On one side were the Central Powers, three empires ruled by authoritarian monarchs: Germany, the Austro-Hungarian Empire, and the Ottoman Empire. On the other side were the Allied Powers. The Allies included Europe's two largest democracies, France and Great Britain. They were joined by Russia, which was ruled by an autocratic monarch, the tsar.

For three years, the United States remained officially neutral in the conflict. Finally, in 1917, the country was drawn into the war on the side

This 1917 poster encourages Americans to purchase war bonds in order to pay for the supplies and training necessary for the U.S. military to participate in World War I and "make the world safe for democracy."

of the Allies. President Woodrow Wilson argued that U.S. involvement in the war was necessary in order to preserve democracy:

> Neutrality is no longer feasible or desirable where the peace of the world is involved and the freedom of its peoples, and the menace to that peace and freedom lies in the existence of autocratic governments backed by organized force which is controlled wholly by their will, not by the will of their people. We have seen the last of neutrality in such circumstances. . . . The world must be made safe for democracy.

In November 1918, the war ended with the defeat of the Central Powers. The conflict and its aftermath swept away empires and monarchs. The Ottoman Empire was gone. The Austro-Hungarian Empire was gone. Germany's emperor, Kaiser Wilhelm II, was forced to give up the throne. Russia's tsar, Nicholas II, was overthrown and executed.

But World War I did not, as President Wilson had hoped, make the world safe for democracy. In many ways, the conflict—and the harsh peace treaty imposed on defeated Germany—paved the way for the biggest threat democracy would ever face: totalitarianism.

6

THE TRIUMPH OF DEMOCRACY?

In the immediate aftermath of World War I, the number of democracies on the globe rose. This was largely a consequence of peace treaties that stripped territory from the defeated Central Powers and created new, democratic states in Europe. By 1920, according to Polity IV data, there were more than 20 democracies in the world.

This blooming of democracy wouldn't last long. Within a few years, an authoritarian backlash was taking shape. Nowhere would the consequences be direr than in Germany. In 1919 a national assembly in Germany wrote a new constitution that set up a democratic federal republic. The constitution guaranteed the basic rights of all German citizens.

But the Weimar Republic, as the new German government was called, proved fragile. Economic woes, bitterness over the harsh peace terms the victorious Allies had imposed on Germany after World War I, and fear of communism combined to create a volatile mix. Political parties that favored democratic governance were unable to put aside their differences. By 1933 Adolf Hitler, leader of the extremist Nazi Party, had exploited the divisions in German society and used street violence—as well as the democratic system itself—to gain power. Hitler quickly put an end to the Weimar Republic and made himself dictator.

In the years after World War I, dictators like Adolf Hitler of Germany and Benito Mussolini of Italy used discontent among the people of their countries, as well as violence and intimidation, to gain power.

In Italy, Benito Mussolini had brought an end to democracy through similar means. Mussolini, leader of the Fascist Party, seized power in a 1922 coup.

Both Hitler and Mussolini held democracy and its ideal of individual rights in utter contempt. They were proponents of totalitarianism, a political system in which the state has unlimited authority and seeks to control virtually every aspect of people's lives.

Totalitarianism had also taken root in another large country. After the overthrow of Russia's tsar in 1917, Communists had won a power struggle and established the Union of Soviet Socialist Republics. Despite this name and an ideology that supposedly promoted economic justice, the Soviet Union was a brutal Communist dictatorship.

THE FIGHT AGAINST TOTALITARIANISM

Throughout the 1930s, Italy, Germany, and another autocratic state, Imperial Japan, carried out various acts of aggression against other

This photograph of Bolshevik leaders Vladimir Lenin (left) and Joseph Stalin was taken in 1922, the year the Union of Soviet Socialist Republics (USSR) was formed. Five years after Lenin's death in 1924, Stalin emerged from a power struggle as the USSR's supreme ruler. During his 23-year dictatorship, the Soviet government deliberately killed between 4 million and 6 million of its own citizens, according to recent estimates by historians.

countries. The world's democracies were unable or unwilling to mount an effective response.

On September 1, 1939, Germany invaded Poland. This finally spurred France and Great Britain to declare war on Germany. These two countries led the Allies, the nations that opposed the Nazis. In 1940 Italy and Japan joined Germany in signing the Axis Pact. It pledged that the three countries would cooperate with one another. Other, smaller nations would also join the Axis Powers.

In June 1940, Germany overran France. This, combined with the Nazis' other conquests and the prewar drift toward authoritarianism, left a mere dozen democracies in the entire world. And the only large power still fighting against the Axis was Britain.

However, in 1941 both the Soviet Union and the United States would join the Allies' cause. The Soviet Union was pulled into the fighting when Germany launched a massive invasion of its territory in June. The United

States entered the conflict in December, after Japanese forces attacked the U.S. naval base at Pearl Harbor, Hawaii.

Humanity paid a horrific price for the ambitions of autocratic leaders in Germany, Italy, and Japan. World War II was the largest conflict in history. It claimed the lives of perhaps 60 million people. The war finally came to an end in September 1945. The Allies—and democracy—had prevailed.

COLD WAR CONSIDERATIONS

In the wake of World War II, the number of democracies in the world again began to rise. U.S. forces occupied defeated Japan, which was reformed along democratic lines. West Germany, occupied by U.S., British, and French forces, also developed into a democracy. In 1947 India gained independence from Great Britain, and within three years the former colony had established a democratic government, becoming the

David Ben-Gurion declares Israel's independence in Tel Aviv, May 14, 1948. Israel's founders intended the new state to be a democracy. Today, it is the only country in the Middle East that the Polity IV Project considers a "full democracy" (the same level as the United States, Great Britain, Australia, and other countries where democratic institutions have long existed).

world's most populous democracy. Israel, a democratic state in the Middle East, was established in 1948. In spite of developments such as these—as well as the European countries' relinquishing of their overseas colonies—the spread of democracy was constrained in the decades following World War II. In large part that was due to the cold war, a bitter struggle for global political dominance between the United States and the Soviet Union. Each superpower tried to enlist other nations to its side, using whatever means necessary.

The Soviet Union, which sought to export communism, set up satellite regimes in most of the countries of Eastern Europe. Communist governments also came to power in countries such as China, North Korea, and Cuba.

While the United States championed a liberal, democratic, and free-market economic system, a determination to prevent the spread of communism often trumped all other considerations. In the eyes of U.S. policymakers, a friendly dictator was preferable to a democratically elected leader with socialist tendencies. In fact, the United States helped overthrow several such leaders during the cold war.

THE THIRD WAVE

A graph of Polity IV data shows democratization reaching a plateau between about 1960 and the mid-1970s. During this time, the number of democracies in the world fluctuated from the low 30s to the mid-30s.

At the same time, a dramatic spike in autocracies can be discerned in the Polity IV graph. Between the late 1950s and the mid-1970s, the number of autocracies in the world more than doubled, to about 90. This largely reflected the decolonization of Africa. After gaining independence from European colonial powers, virtually every African country fell into authoritarian rule.

An upswing in democratization began in the mid-1970s, gathered momentum through the 1980s, and surged after 1989. In the early 1990s Samuel P. Huntington, an influential American political scientist, labeled this trend democracy's third wave. The first wave, he said, lasted from the early 1800s (when the United States expanded voting rights to include nearly all white men) to 1922 (when Mussolini seized power in Italy). The second wave lasted from the end of World War II (when democracies were restored in parts of Europe) to 1962 (when the number of democracies began to decline from a peak of 36, according to Huntington). Huntington dated the third wave to 1974, when Portugal's longtime dictatorship was overthrown.

By the early 1990s, the third wave had swept away authoritarian regimes in southern Europe, East Asia, Latin America, and Eastern Europe. Huntington proposed several major causes for this trend. Some authoritarian regimes couldn't maintain their legitimacy in the face of economic failures and military defeats. Others were undermined by economic development, which led to greater levels of education and a growing middle class—factors, that, Huntington said, produce increased demands for political rights. The third wave of democratization, Huntington argued, also gained momentum from the "snowballing" phenomenon. This describes the positive example, for people still living under an authoritarian regime, set by a country that has successfully transitioned to democracy.

Huntington also pointed to the role policy changes in the United States and the Soviet Union played in fostering democracy. Promoting human rights worldwide became an explicit

While presenting itself as a champion of democracy during the Cold War, the U.S. government sometimes worked to eliminate democratically elected leaders of other countries that were perceived as friendly to the Soviet Union. One of them was Salvador Allende, a socialist who was elected president of Chile in 1970. With secret U.S. support, a coup toppled Allende from power in 1973. General Augusto Pinochet, the leader of the coup, subsequently ruled Chile as a dictator until 1990. His regime arrested, tortured, and executed tens of thousands of political opponents.

The fact that a country holds democratic elections is no guarantee that democracy will flourish there. In June 2012, Egyptians elected Mohammed Morsi as the country's president. Egypt is attempting to make a transition to a democratic government after decades of autocratic rule, and Morsi has said that he supports key principles of democracy, such as allowing people the right to meet and demonstrate peacefully or criticize the government, establishing an independent judiciary, and holding fair elections. However, many international observers are concerned because Morsi represents the Muslim Brotherhood, an organization that has expressed the goal of establishing Islamic religious law as the basis for Egypt's government and society.

foreign-policy goal during the administration of U.S. president Jimmy Carter (1977–81). Carter's successor, Ronald Reagan, was arguably less concerned about human rights. But he did focus on promoting democratic change through diplomatic, economic, and in some cases, military pressure.

In the Soviet Union, Mikhail Gorbachev—who came to power in 1985—introduced political and economic reforms. In 1989 Gorbachev announced that the Soviet Union would no longer maintain Communist dictatorships in the countries of Eastern Europe. Instead it would permit these countries to decide their own internal affairs. One Communist regime after another was swept from power in favor of democracy. In 1991 the Soviet Union itself disintegrated. The cold war was over, and the number of democracies in the world was skyrocketing.

LIBERAL DEMOCRACY: INEVITABLE?

Huntington noted that each of the first two waves of democratization had been followed by a reverse wave of authoritarianism. He didn't say that democracy's third wave was irreversible.

That, however, is essentially what Francis Fukuyama implied. In 1992 Fukuyama published a book titled *The End of History and the Last Man*. In it he argued that the failure of communism left liberal democracy as the only viable form of government. Democracy's triumph in the long run, Fukuyama said, was inevitable. At some point in the future, all governments would be democratic.

The idea didn't seem too outlandish in the 1990s. By 1999 Freedom House counted 120 electoral democracies, up from 76 in 1990, and just 39 in 1974.

But during the first decade of the 21st century, democracy's worldwide momentum appeared to stall, with countries such as Russia, Venezuela, Nigeria, and Thailand becoming significantly more authoritarian.

Meanwhile, terrorism presented new challenges for well-established liberal democracies. Nearly 3,000 Americans were killed in the al-Qaeda attacks of September 11, 2001. More than 190 people died in Madrid, Spain, when Islamist terrorists targeted the train system in 2004. The following year, London's transit system was hit by coordinated bombings. This time the death toll exceeded 50.

Liberal democratic governments grappled with the problem of how to prevent terrorism while still protecting civil liberties. Many observers noted significant erosion of civil liberties, especially in the United States.

"It is not easy to build a sturdy democracy," noted a 2010 report by the Economist Intelligence Unit. "Even in long-established ones, if not nurtured and protected, democracy can corrode."

Democracy is often difficult and messy. Democratic governments can be exasperatingly slow to act. At times they seem paralyzed by the competing demands of different parties and interest groups.

Still, democracy has historically proved flexible, adaptable, and responsive. The British statesman Winston Churchill once summed up democracy's enduring appeal. "Democracy is the worst form of Government," Churchill said, "except all those other forms that have been tried from time to time."

CHAPTER NOTES

p. 12: "I would rather be exposed . . ." Thomas Jefferson, letter to Archibald Stuart, December 23, 1791. *The Thomas Jefferson Papers*, Library of Congress. http://memory.loc.gov/cgi-bin/query/r?ammem/mtj:@field(DOCID+@lit(tj060178))

p. 22–23: "The laws of nature . . ." Thomas Collett Sandars (ed.), *The Institutes of Justinian; with English Introduction, Translation, and Notes* (London: J. W. Parker and Son, 1853), p. 94.

p. 25: "No free man shall . . ." Jon E. Lewis (ed.), *A Documentary History of Human Rights: A Record of the Events, Documents and Speeches That Shaped Our World* (Philadelphia: Running Press, 2003), p. 145.

p. 25: "Except for a tiny handful . . ." John Keane, *The Life and Death of Democracy* (New York: W.W. Norton and Co., 2009), p. 4.

p. 31: "When the legislative . . ." Charles de Secondat, Baron de Montesquieu, *The Spirit of the Laws*, 1748. Modern History Sourcebook. http://www.fordham.edu/halsall/mod/montesquieu-spirit.asp

p. 34: "We hold these Truths . . ." Declaration of Independence. http://www.archives.gov/exhibits/charters/declaration_transcript.html

p. 35: "There is but one rank . . ." Constitution of Pennsylvania—September 28, 1776. http://avalon.law.yale.edu/18th_century/pa08.asp

p. 38: "The people are the King," John R. Vile, *The Constitutional Convention of 1787: A Comprehensive Encyclopedia of America's Founding* (Santa Barbara, CA: ABC-CLIO, 2005), p. 283.

p. 39: "most likely to possess . . ." [Alexander Hamilton], *The Federalist*, No. 68. http://www.constitution.org/fed/federa68.htm

p. 39: "A republic, madam . . ." Walter Isaacson, *Benjamin Franklin: An American Life* (New York: Simon & Schuster, 2003), p. 459.

p. 41: "Men are born and remain . . ." Declaration of the Rights of Man and the Citizen. http://www.hrcr.org/docs/frenchdec.html

p. 42: "We have been beaten . . ." Frank W. Thackeray and John E. Findling (eds.), *Events that Changed the World in the Nineteenth Century* (Westport, CT: Greenwood Publishing, 1996), p. 84.

p. 45: "choice was limited . . ." Organization for Security and Co-operation in Europe, "Russia's presidential election marked by unequal campaign conditions, active citizens' engagement, international observers say" (March 5, 2012). http://www.osce.org/odihr/elections/88661

p. 49: "Neutrality is no longer feasible . . ." Woodrow Wilson, speech to U.S. Senate, January 22, 1917. In *My Fellow Americans: The Most Important Speeches of America's Presidents, from George Washington to Barack Obama*, edited by Michael Waldman (Naperville, IL: 2010), p. 84.

p. 57: "It is not easy to build . . ." Democracy Index 2010. London: Economist Intelligence Unit, 2010. http://graphics.eiu.com/PDF/Democracy_Index_2010_web.pdf

p. 57: "Democracy is the worst . . ." Winston Churchill, speech to the House of Commons, November 11, 1947. Quoted in *The Wicked Wit of Winston Churchill*, compiled by Dominique Enright (London: Michael O'Mara Books Ltd., 2001), p. 5.

The Greek city-state of Athens is considered the birthplace of democracy.

CHRONOLOGY

CA. 3RD MILLENNIUM BCE: Mesopotamian city-states have assemblies.

5TH–4TH BCE: Direct democracy flourishes in Athens and other Greek city-states.

1100 CE: King Henry I of England issues the Charter of Liberties.

1215: England's King John is forced to sign the Magna Carta.

1295: England's Kind Edward I calls the "Model Parliament," a council that includes commoners.

1642–51: The English Civil War, during which Parliamentary forces overthrow the monarchy.

1660: The English monarchy is restored.

1688–89: England's "Glorious Revolution": King James II is overthrown by William of Orange; Parliament passes Bill of Rights.

1775: The Revolutionary War begins on April 19 with battles at Lexington and Concord, Massachusetts.

1776: The Continental Congress adopts the Declaration of Independence on July 4.

1783: The Treaty of Paris officially ends the Revolutionary War; Great Britain recognizes American independence.

1787: The Constitutional Convention meets in Philadelphia and produces the Constitution of the United States.

1788: The U.S. Constitution is ratified.

1789: The French Revolution begins.

1791: The Bill of Rights is added to the U.S. Constitution.

1799: Napoleon Bonaparte seizes control of France's republican government, turns it into a dictatorship.

1832: Britain passes First Reform Act, increasing citizens' voting rights.

1870: African-American males are eligible to vote in the United States.

1918: All adult males are eligible to vote in Britain.

1920: All adult women can vote in the United States.

1928: Women win the right to vote in Britain.

1939–45: World War II.

1950: India formally adopts a constitution; becomes the world's most populous democracy.

1989: The Soviet Union relinquishes control of Eastern Europe.

1991: The Soviet Union collapses, paving the way for a wave of democratization.

2012: About half of the world's nations have governments that operate as full or partial democracies.

GLOSSARY

ARISTOCRACY—government by a small, privileged class; a governing body or ruling class made up of a hereditary nobility.

AUTHORITARIAN—relating to or characteristic of a regime in which obedience to the ruling power is expected.

AUTOCRATIC—having unlimited power.

CIVIL LIBERTIES—fundamental rights and freedoms guaranteed to citizens.

CONSTITUTION—the basic laws and principles of a nation; a written document specifying the structure and rules of a government.

CONSTITUENT—someone who is represented by an elected official.

DESPOT—a ruler with absolute power; a tyrant.

FRANCHISE—the right to vote.

IDEOLOGY—a system of political and social beliefs.

OLIGARCHY—a government in which a small group exercises control, often for corrupt ends.

REPRESENTATIVE DEMOCRACY—a form of government under which people choose others to act on their behalf.

REPUBLIC—a government in which supreme power rests with the body of citizens entitled to vote and that has elected legislators and an elected head of state.

SOVEREIGN—having supreme or ultimate authority.

SUFFRAGE—the right to vote.

FURTHER READING

Campbell, Heather M., ed. *Advances in Democracy: From the French Revolution to the Present-Day European Union.* New York: Rosen, 2011.

Davenport, John C. *Democracy in the Middle East.* New York: Chelsea House, 2007.

Faiella, Graham. *John Locke: Champion of Modern Democracy.* New York: Rosen, 2005.

Fitzpatrick, Anne. *Democracy.* Mankato, MN: Creative Education, 2008.

Lansford, Tom. *Democracy (Global Viewpoints).* Detroit: Greenhaven Press, 2011.

Stites, Bill. *Democracy: A Primary Source Analysis.* New York: Rosen, 2003.

Vander Hook, Sue. *Democracy.* Edina, MN: ABDO Publishing, 2011.

Woolf, Alex. *Democracy.* Milwaukee, WI: World Almanac Library, 2006.

INTERNET RESOURCES

http://www.icpd.org/democracy/index.htm

An essay on the development of democracy in Western Europe, presented by the International Center for Peace and Development.

http://www.historyworld.net/wrldhis/PlainTextHistories.asp?historyid=ac42

This site traces the development of democracy from the ancient Greeks, through medieval times, and into its modern manifestations.

http://www.bbc.co.uk/history/ancient/greeks/greekdemocracy_01.shtml

This page examines the institution of democracy in ancient Greece, discussing how it operated and how it compares to modern democracies.

http://history-world.org/french_revolution.htm

An account of the French Revolution, describing its causes, events, and outcomes, and how it affected the development of democracy in Europe.

http://europeandemocracy.org/

The European Foundation for Democracy promotes freedom and equality for all of Europe's citizens, and examines current issues that it considers a threat to those principles.

INDEX

Numbers in **bold italics** refer to captions.

CONTRIBUTORS

Senior Consulting Editor TIMOTHY J. COLTON is Morris and Anna Feldberg Professor of Government and Russian Studies and is the chair of the Department of Government at Harvard University. His books include *The Dilemma of Reform in the Soviet Union* (1986); *Moscow: Governing the Socialist Metropolis* (1995), which was named best scholarly book in government and political science by the Association of American Publishers; *Transitional Citizens: Voters and What Influences Them in the New Russia* (2000); and *Popular Choice and Managed Democracy: The Russian Elections of 1999 and 2000* (with Michael McFaul, 2003). Dr. Colton is a member of the editorial board of World Politics and Post-Soviet Affairs.

DIANE BAILEY has written more than twenty nonfiction books for children and teens, on topics ranging from sports to states. She also writes fiction, and looks forward to the release of her first murder mystery novel in 2012. As a freelance editor, Diane works to help authors who write fiction for children and young adults. With her two sons and two dogs, Diane lives in Kansas.